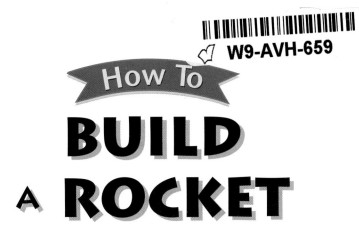

How To

BUILD
A ROCKET

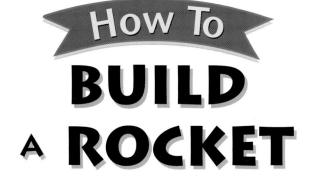

How To
BUILD
A ROCKET

By HAZEL RICHARDSON

Illustrated by
Scoular Anderson

FRANKLIN WATTS
A Division of Scholastic Inc.
New York Toronto London Auckland Sydney
Mexico City New Delhi Hong Kong
Danbury, Connecticut

For my father, the original mad inventor

First published 1999 by Oxford University Press
Great Clarendon Street, Oxford OX2 6DP

First American edition 2001 by Franklin Watts
A Division of Scholastic Inc.
90 Sherman Turnpike
Danbury, CT 06816

Catalog details are available from the Library of Congress Cataloging-in-Publication Data

ISBN 0-531-14643-X (lib. bdg.) 0-531-13998-0 (pbk.)

Printed in China

Contents

Introduction

Why Build a Rocket?   6

Chapter One

What Is the Moon?   9

Chapter Two

The Gravity Guys   28

Chapter Three

Trying to Get to the Moon   36

Chapter Four

A Rocket to the Moon   44

Chapter Five

The Space Race   67

Chapter Six

Blast Off on Your Moon Mission   81

WHY BUILD A ROCKET?

On July 20, 1969, Neil Armstrong climbed down the ladder of his lunar module in his bulky spacesuit and took humankind's first steps on the moon. People had dreamed about this moment for thousands of years. Armstrong's words are probably the most famous ever spoken. Most people think he said, "That's one small step for man, one giant leap for mankind," because the "a" got lost in the radio transmission.

This giant leap was possible because we had finally figured out how to build a rocket that would get us to the moon. It took thousands of years, and the work of the world's most brilliant scientists, to build a rocket powerful enough to propel us out of Earth's atmosphere and protect the brave astronauts inside from the deadly effects of space:

1. There is no air in space. If something makes a hole in your spacesuit or rocket, your eyeballs will be sucked out.

2. In space it can either be icy, deathly cold, or so hot that you would fry without protection.

3. Space is a zero-gravity environment. This means you are weightless, so it is difficult to move. (Astronauts who come back to Earth after a long time in space find it difficult to keep their balance.) Weightlessness also does horrible things to your body:

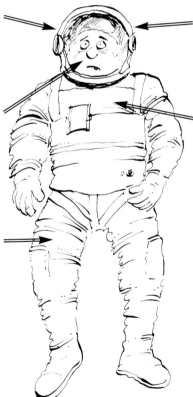

Your head moves around all over the place, which makes you feel dizzy and sick.

Your face gets puffy and swollen. (No rocket romance for you!) Your nose feels all plugged up because of the fluid in your head.

Your bones stop growing. Astronauts who come back to Earth after spending a lot of time in zero-gravity find that their bones break easily.

Blood collects in your head and chest because gravity isn't pulling it down.

Your heart shrinks because it doesn't have to work as hard as on Earth, and your muscles waste away.

4. There are asteroids, meteorites, and pieces of old satellites flying about in space—not to mention deadly radiation, and Earth's atmosphere waiting to burn you up if you fall into it at the wrong time.

Aside from all the dangers of traveling through space, it is very difficult to survive on the moon. Your rocket has to carry all your food, fuel, clothing, and equipment, as well as large quantities of air to breathe.

In 1998, scientists were delighted to discover over 300 million tons of frozen water on the moon. This means NASA's long-term objective of setting up a moon base is more likely to happen in the future.

If you want to go to the moon, you need to build a rocket to get you there. You also need to know what you are getting yourself into. It's a trip only the bravest can make! This book will help. It will tell you all about

 what the moon is, how far away it is, and how it was made

 the silly ideas people used to have about the moon and space travel

how rockets were invented

why it is so difficult for us to get to the moon

 how to make your own space suit

how to build a working rocket

what to take with you when you travel to the moon

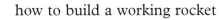

CHAPTER ONE

WHAT IS THE MOON?

The moon is a dusty ball of rock about a quarter of the size of Earth. It circles the Earth about once a month in a path called an orbit. Because the moon orbits around us, it is called our satellite.

The moon is a dangerous place—there is no air to breathe, and it can get as cold as -275°F (-170°C) at night. Brrr!

-275°? That's even colder than our classroom in winter!

People have always wanted to go to the moon, even when they didn't know what it was. In the future, the moon could be very useful to us. The U.S. space agency NASA wants to set up a moon base in this century. The base could be used as a launchpad for missions to other planets. We could also mine rocks on the moon and dump waste that is harmful here on Earth. Of course, the people living in the moon base might not be too happy about that!

Here are some amazing moon facts:

The moon is 2,160 miles (3,476 kilometers) across.

The moon is about 242,300 miles (390,000 km) away from us.

There is no weather on the moon (more about this later).

Lots of other planets in the solar system also have moons.

The moon gives us light at night.

The moon makes the seas move and gives us tides.

The moon helped ancient peoples measure time.

Since civilization began, people have stared up into the night sky and watched the moon and the stars moving. In ancient times, people didn't know what they were. They came up with some amazing (but inaccurate) explanations about what the moon and stars are, why they move, and why the moon changes shape.

Babylonian Baloney

About 1500 B.C., a Babylonian astronomer declared, "The moon and stars are where the gods live. The sky is just an arch stretching over the Earth. When we look at the moon, it's like looking in through a god's window."

Even though they had funny ideas, the Babylonians correctly observed that the moon and stars move around in the sky. They also discovered that the planets move at different speeds.

The Babylonians thought the movements of the moon and stars were messages from the gods, so they spent most nights staring up at the sky to try and read the messages. This started the ancient art of astrology. Even today, you can read in the newspaper what it means for your future when a particular star wanders across the sky.

The Egyptian Explanation ....

Other ancient peoples, such as the Egyptians, had ideas different from those of the Babylonians.

The moon changes shape because a pig nibbles at it and sometimes gobbles it all up!

Of course, the ancient Egyptians were wrong. A pig is not gobbling the moon up every month! But you can see why they might have thought so when you do the following experiment to see what happens to the moon's shape.

13

Be a Rocket Scientist
SEE HOW THE MOON SEEMS TO CHANGE SHAPE

WHAT YOU'LL NEED
- some paper and pens/pencils
- your eyes!

WHAT TO DO
1. Stand outside (or look out your window) on a night when it isn't cloudy. Look at the moon, draw its shape, and write down the date. (If you can't see the moon, write down that you can't see it, along with the date.)
2. Every night for a month, look at the moon and draw its shape.

WHAT HAPPENS?
Every month, the moon changes shape lots of times. It starts off as a big circle—a full moon (if you're superstitious, watch out for those werewolves!). Then it gets smaller and smaller, until it vanishes. Finally, it grows back into a full moon.

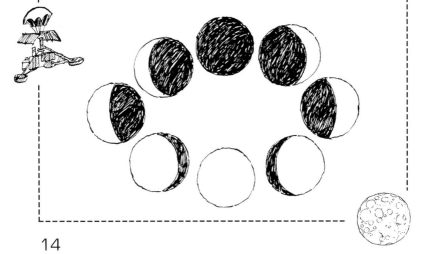

Mooning Around ....

The moon doesn't really change shape at all. It just *looks* like it's changing shape because of the way sunlight falls on it as it moves around us. The moon reflects the light back at us like a dusty mirror. You can see what happens in this experiment.

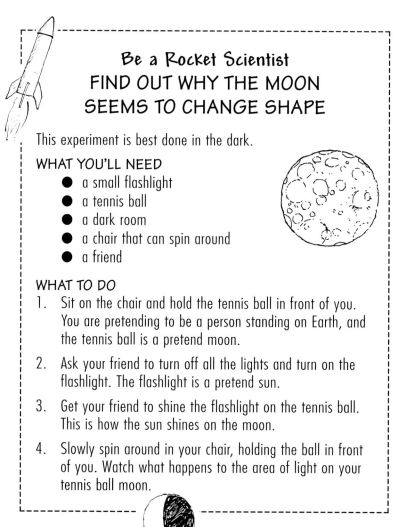

Be a Rocket Scientist
FIND OUT WHY THE MOON SEEMS TO CHANGE SHAPE

This experiment is best done in the dark.

WHAT YOU'LL NEED
- a small flashlight
- a tennis ball
- a dark room
- a chair that can spin around
- a friend

WHAT TO DO
1. Sit on the chair and hold the tennis ball in front of you. You are pretending to be a person standing on Earth, and the tennis ball is a pretend moon.

2. Ask your friend to turn off all the lights and turn on the flashlight. The flashlight is a pretend sun.

3. Get your friend to shine the flashlight on the tennis ball. This is how the sun shines on the moon.

4. Slowly spin around in your chair, holding the ball in front of you. Watch what happens to the area of light on your tennis ball moon.

WHAT HAPPENS?

As you spin around, the moon is sometimes between the flashlight and you, and you cannot see it. As it moves around, you can see more and more of it because more and more light falls on it. This is how the moon appears to change shape.

Greek Guesses................................

None of the ancient peoples were able to figure out that the moon didn't really change shape. Even when the ancient Greeks came along—and they were very clever—they couldn't make up their minds about why the moon changed shape. (Perhaps this was because they didn't have swivel chairs to experiment with.) Some Greeks thought the moon was another big lump of rock like the Earth. This was the right idea, but others weren't convinced.

Other Greek scientists, such as Posidonius, had different ideas.

Anaximander, who lived in the sixth century B.C., disagreed yet again.

Anaximander was a clever man. He was one of the first people to figure out that stars are actually great balls of fire. He was wrong about the moon being made of fire, though.

The arguments about the moon were only solved when the telescope was invented and people could get a close look at it. Everyone then agreed that the moon shines because it reflects light from the sun.

The Man in the Moon..........................

If you look at the full moon, you'll see dark splotches on it that look like a face. People used to imagine that there was a man in the moon.

It was the work of Galileo Galilei, one of the greatest scientists ever, that proved there wasn't a man in the moon after all.

Galileo Gets a Close-Up
Italy, 1609

When Galileo Galilei heard about a newfangled instrument called an optical tube (that's a telescope to you and me), he knew it would be just the thing to help him find out more about the moon. It took him years to figure out how to build his own telescope. When he finally succeeded, he found he could make things look four hundred times bigger than they did before! Now he could see what was really on the moon.

Galileo was amazed.

It looks just like the Earth! The light parts are land, and the darker blobs are seas...

When other astronomers heard about Galileo's discovery, they rushed to look at this marvelous new world. They all agreed with him. They began to draw maps of the moon and even said they could see trees and deformed moon animals wandering around.

But Galileo was wrong. There are no beautiful seas on the moon. The dark blobs he saw were actually horrible dark craters. There are over 3 trillion of them, and the biggest one is about 185 miles (295 km) wide and 2.5 miles (4 km) deep!

Because Galileo and other early astronomers thought the moon was like Earth, they gave some of the places on it very silly names. See if you can guess which of these names are real places on the moon.

- Sea of Rains
- Lake of Dreams
- The Lunar Alps
- Bay of Rainbows
- Sea of Tranquillity

Answer: they all are!

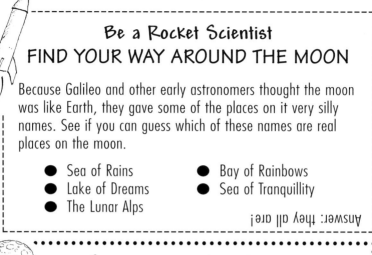

The Moon Is Born
Italy, 1609

Most scientists think there are no seas on the moon, and it is pockmarked with huge craters, because the moon used to be a piece of Earth until a terrifying accident sent it spinning off into space. To see what really happened, we have to go back in time more than five billion years...

Earth, and the other planets in the solar system, have just formed from a ball of red-hot gas. There is no life here yet—which is a very good thing, because something devastating is about to happen. Looming in the distance and heading straight for us is a lump of rock the size of the planet Mars.

When the lump of rock hits the Earth, the result is disastrous. Whole pieces of the Earth go spinning into space, along with the guilty planet that hit us.

The lumps of rock are trapped in orbit around the Earth.
Gradually, they bang into one another and stick together.
After about 500 million years, the rocks cool and the moon is
born.

Congratulations!
It's the moon!

Meteorite Mayhem ....

It's a good thing for us that the moon was created, because we might not be here otherwise! Ever since the solar system formed, there have been millions of bits of rock floating around all over the place. Most of the time, these bits of rock just zoom around the sun, not getting in anyone's way. But every so often, their paths cross with the orbit of one of the planets. The gravity of the planet helps pull the rock toward it. This could cause a disaster if one hit Earth—and maybe even wipe us out completely! Luckily, the moon orbits the Earth very quickly and also has some gravity. This means that a rock headed toward us is more likely to hit the moon.

Scientists think the Earth was hit by a massive meteorite 65 million years ago. It hurtled into the Earth's atmosphere and ended up falling on Mexico. It left a crater 125 miles (200 km) wide and threw clouds of poisonous dust and gas into the air that blocked out the sunlight and affected the weather. Some scientists believe this is what might have killed off the dinosaurs. If a really large meteorite hit the Earth today, it could kill all of us as well. So you can see how lucky it is that most meteorites hit the moon and not us!

Smashed-up meteorites that have hit the moon are scattered all over its surface as dusty rubble. Even today, the moon is hit by 70 to 150 meteorites a year. Some of them weigh up to 2,200 pounds (1,000 kilograms)! If we are going to build a moon base, we need to find some way of protecting it from falling meteorites. Scientists think the best way might be to build the moon base in underground tunnels.

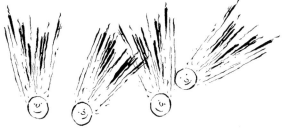

Weathering Meteorite Showers ....

Even though meteorites could crash down on your head, one reason why you might want to go to the moon is that it never rains there—or snows, or hails, or has hurricanes! Why? Because of the force of gravity.

Gravity is what keeps your feet on the ground. It also keeps the atmosphere on Earth from floating off into space. The moon is smaller than the Earth, so it has less gravity—not enough to hold an atmosphere. This means you have to take your own air supply with you when you visit—and hope you don't run out!

No air means no weather, either. Wind is moving air, and clouds only form when invisible water vapor in the air cools to form tiny droplets. If these droplets get big enough, rain falls. On Earth this usually happens when air moves high into the atmosphere and cools down. You can make this happen at home.

Be a Rocket Scientist
SEE WHY THERE IS
NO WEATHER ON THE MOON

Have an adult help you with this experiment.

WHAT YOU'LL NEED

- a glass jar with a wide neck
- a rubber glove with no holes
- a box of matches
- some water

WHAT TO DO

1. Cover the bottom of the jar with a thin layer of water.
2. Drop a lit match into the jar. (This makes smoke, which you'll need in order to see the cloud you are going to make.)
3. Put the rubber glove partly inside the jar, with the fingers hanging down inside. Stretch the top of the glove over the mouth of the jar to make a seal.

4. Put your hand into the glove and pull it up quickly, being careful not to pull the glove off the bottle. What happens?

5. Now repeat the experiment with no water in the bottle (but clean and dry the bottle and the glove first). Does the same thing happen?

WHAT HAPPENS?

Some of the water you have put in the jar evaporates and turns into water vapor. When you pull the glove up, you make the air in the jar spread out. This makes it cool down. You make a cloud in the bottle! When there is no water in the bottle, no cloud forms. This is why there is no rain on the moon.

CHAPTER TWO

THE GRAVITY GUYS

After maps had been drawn of the amazing moon, covered with beautiful seas with strange names, people were very excited to go and visit. But this was easier said than done. The moon is thousands of miles away, through the deadly vacuum of space—without a service station in sight.

The main problem is getting off the Earth in the first place. Gravity holds us on the Earth so strongly that it takes enormous force to get anything into space. If your rocket is not powerful enough, you'll be pulled back to Earth and squashed into tiny pieces.

Most of our information about gravity was gathered by three scientists. The first person to study why things are pulled down to the ground was an ancient Greek (yes, another one!) named Aristotle.

Everything is made up of earth, water, fire, or air. Each of these things has a place where it likes to be. So, a stone falls because it has earth in it, and earth belongs on the ground. Oww!

This sounds silly now, but people believed this idea for almost two thousand years. Then in Italy in 1586, Simon Stevinus came along and did a very famous experiment. (Well, he said it was an experiment, but it was probably an accident when he was bumped from behind by a tourist.) Stevinus was at the top of a tower when he dropped the two things he was holding, and they fell over the edge. We don't know what these things were. But we do know that even though they had different weights, they hit the ground at the same time.

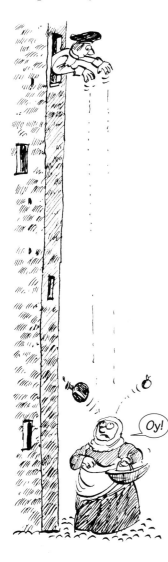

Oy!

Remember Galileo, the world's greatest scientist? Well, he couldn't bear for someone to discover something he didn't know about. He repeated Stevinus's experiment and also started rolling balls down slopes to see what happened to them. He concluded that as something fell, it speeded up. But even he couldn't explain why. In the end, he gave up in disgust.

Newton's News ....

The top gravity guy was Isaac Newton.

It's 1665, the year of the Black Death. People all over Europe are developing horrible black lumps on their bodies and dropping dead like flies. Isaac Newton has been sent home from Cambridge University in England to escape the plague. One day he is sitting in his garden at Woolsthorpe Manor, wondering what keeps the moon going around the Earth. Suddenly, an apple falls to the ground, and he has a brilliant idea.

Newton called his idea the Universal Law of Gravitation. It explained lots of things, including

- why heavy things fall on your toes
- why the seas move in tides every day
- why the moon doesn't shoot off into space

The moon circles the Earth because of gravity! It's the same force that pulls an apple to the ground.

Be a Rocket Scientist
SEE HOW GRAVITY MAKES THE MOON ORBIT EARTH

Although the Earth's gravity pulls the moon toward it, the moon doesn't hit the Earth because it is moving so quickly. The speed of the moon keeps it moving in a circular orbit. You can see how this works in a very simple experiment.

WHAT YOU'LL NEED

● a long piece of string

● a plastic ball about the size of a marble

● some space outside

WHAT TO DO

1. Attach the plastic ball to the end of the piece of string. The plastic ball is your moon, and the string is imaginary gravity.
2. Stand with the loose end of string in your hand and spin around. You are the Earth spinning.
3. Watch what happens to the plastic moon. Then try spinning the plastic moon faster and slower. What happens?
4. Make sure no one is around, and let go of the moon. What happens?

What on Earth is going on?

WHAT HAPPENS?

The plastic moon wants to go off in a straight line, but it can't. It doesn't get any closer to you because it is moving very fast.

If you let go of the string, the plastic moon shoots off in a straight line. Without gravity, this is what would happen to the moon. It would shoot off in a straight line and disappear into space.

Gravity is also what keeps the Earth in orbit around the sun.

All Washed Up! . . . .

Newton could also explain why the seas move up and down every day. It's because the pull of the moon's gravity on the seas creates bulges, so that the sea level is higher in some places than in others.

Be a Rocket Scientist
SEE HOW GRAVITY MOVES THE SEA

Gravity is a pulling force. It is impossible for you to create gravity yourself. Instead, by creating another pulling force called electrostatic attraction, you can see how gravity pulls water toward the moon. Electrostatic attraction happens when something has an electric charge.

WHAT YOU'LL NEED
- a running faucet
- a balloon
- a wool sweater

WHAT TO DO
1. Blow up the balloon. This is going to be your moon.
2. Give the balloon an electric charge by rubbing it quickly (and carefully, so that it doesn't pop!) against the sweater.
3. Turn the faucet on and hold the balloon close to the water. What happens?

WHAT HAPPENS?
The water moves toward the balloon! This is similar to what happens when gravity from the moon pulls on the seas.

Planet Power ....

When Newton said that everything had gravity, he meant everything. Even you have gravity!

The problem is that gravity is a very weak force, and you're not big enough to pull things toward you. Sorry! It's only when something is as big as a moon or a planet that we start to feel the gravitational force.

Even though gravity is a weak force, Earth is so large that we can't beat its gravitational pull by ourselves. To get to the moon, we need something that can defeat the force of gravity and fly for thousands of miles without needing to refuel—something people tried to find for thousands of years…

CHAPTER THREE

TRYING TO GET TO THE MOON

Ever since the ancient Greeks discovered that the moon was not a lump of green cheese but a big lump of rock, people have dreamed of getting there. Before the twentieth century this was impossible, because nobody had even figured out how to get off the ground and stay up in the air. But that didn't stop them. People still came up with lots of amazing ideas for how they might get to the moon—and what would happen when they did.

Traveler's Tales

The first stories about traveling to the moon were written by the ancient Greek (yes, yet another one!) Lucian in A.D. 160. He had two ideas for getting there: first, being snatched up by a whirlwind; and second, by fastening a vulture's wing to one shoulder and an eagle's wing to the other, then flying there.

Spaceships? Nah! Who needs 'em? Eat your heart out, Captain Kirk!

Our hero didn't stop when he got to the moon. He also traveled to Venus and some of the stars!

Spaced Out ....

After Lucian's tales, no more space travel stories were written for hundreds of years. This was mostly because the Christian church didn't want anybody writing about different worlds. But when Lucian's stories were published again in the seventeenth century, it inspired people to try again.

One of these new books by Johannes Kepler was published in 1634, after he had died. Kepler was an astronomer, so his book was less silly than Lucian's.

What he got right:	People traveling in space feel weightless and have problems breathing.
	Night on the moon lasts for fifteen to sixteen days.
What he got wrong:	The moon is full of snakelike animals and plants. Every day they grow to huge sizes, and when the sun goes down they hide underground or die!

Bishops Blast Off into Space.................

Two important books were written in 1638 by bishops. *The Man in the Moone* was written by Francis Godwin. He claimed people could get to the moon by tying themselves to wild swans.

Bishop John Wilkins's book was called *The Discovery of a World in the Moone*.

What he got right: People are weightless in space.

What he got wrong: People in space do not need food or sleep.
People can get to the moon in a flying chariot.

Astronauts Ahoy!...............................

Soon everyone was trying to design a spaceship to take them to the moon. In 1650, the famous Frenchman Cyrano de Bergerac (also famous for his big nose) came up with several ideas.

40

Rocket Man

People may have laughed at these ideas, but de Bergerac had indeed hit on the right one—rockets! It's the Earth's gravity that makes it so difficult to get to the moon. Gravity is useful for holding us down on the ground, but it's hard to beat. To escape from its clutches completely, you need to reach a speed of over 6 miles (10 km) per second! Rockets are the only thing we have that can beat the force of gravity and break out of the Earth's atmosphere. Even the modern space shuttle uses rockets to launch it into space.

How Does a Rocket Work?

You might think that because rockets are powerful enough to take a metal can full of humans and equipment to the moon and back, they must be very complicated. In fact, they're so simple, even a baby could understand how they work.

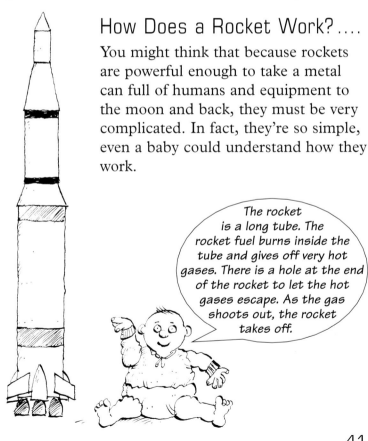

The rocket is a long tube. The rocket fuel burns inside the tube and gives off very hot gases. There is a hole at the end of the rocket to let the hot gases escape. As the gas shoots out, the rocket takes off.

Be a Rocket Scientist
SEE HOW A ROCKET WORKS

WHAT YOU'LL NEED

● a balloon

WHAT TO DO

1. Blow up the balloon.
2. Let go of it!

PHWAAARGH!

WHAT HAPPENS?

The air in the balloon rushes out of the hole at the end and pushes the balloon away. This is just how a rocket moves.

Over the years, people have come up with many different ways to use rockets—some very strange, some very dangerous, some useful, and some just for fun…

CHAPTER FOUR

A ROCKET TO THE MOON

Nobody knows for sure when rockets were first invented, but most people think the Chinese invented them in the first century A.D. They found rockets very useful as weapons.

The Mad History of Rockets
Part I: Kai-beng, China; 1232

Kai-fung-fu is a Chinese town in terror. Hordes of Mongol horsemen have surrounded the town and are just waiting for their chance to attack. The brave soldiers defending this town are outnumbered... Oh no! The Mongols are attacking!

But what's this? The Mongols are being driven back by what look like arrows of fire. I don't believe it! They've attached little rockets to their arrows! The arrows are zooming around at high speed and exploding just like fireworks.

The Mongols are terrified. To make things worse, they're having gunpowder bombs dropped on their heads as well. They're in retreat! The rocket arrows have saved the day!

The Mad History of Rockets

Part II:

China, 1420

Wan Hu, a well-known official, has decided to see if he can use rockets to fly. He's built an amazing flying machine out of two kites with a seat fastened underneath. His flying machine is going to be powered by 47—yes, that's 47—rockets, and 47 assistants are standing by, ready to light each of the rockets at the same time.

Wan Hu is climbing into his seat. His assistants are getting ready. The tension is unbearable... Oh! He's given the signal! The assistants are rushing in with their torches...

BLAM!

Oh my goodness! What an explosion!

And Wan Hu was never seen again. This story was probably why people didn't try using rockets to fly again for a long time.

Rockets Are All the Rage!....................

In the 1800s, bombarding Napoleon with rockets saved England from being invaded by the French. Apart from war, people thought rockets weren't of much use for anything except fireworks displays. But some scientists and inventors were still impressed with the speed of rockets and thought there must be something else they could do with them. They came up with some incredible rocket inventions:

 a rocket plane (which didn't fly)

 getting rid of storm clouds by firing rockets into them

lifting spy cameras into the sky on rockets and bringing them back down by parachute (this worked very well)

rocket-propelled cars

mail delivery by rocket

I thought my new mail-delivery idea would really take off!

Rockets were soon to have their day. At the beginning
of the twentieth century, a Swedish rocket scientist
named Wilhelm Unge announced to the world that he
had developed an "aerial torpedo." He had improved
the old war rockets, which could only fly for a couple
of miles with the power of nitroglycerine. (This is the
stuff that dynamite is made of, so you can imagine
how far and fast Unge's rockets flew!) Unge thought
his rockets would be useful for shooting down any hot
air balloons that happened to sail over his garden. The
Germans agreed with him and bought some to
experiment with. They came in very useful during the
war, when hot-air balloons were used to try to see
behind enemy lines.

World War II saw researchers from all over the world fighting among themselves to see who could make the most powerful rocket weapons. The German scientists started the war in the lead with a rocket called the Nebelwerfer. The British and U.S. troops called it the Screaming Meemie because of the dreadful screeching noise it made as it came in to land. The Americans answered back with the bazooka, a handheld rocket launcher. The Germans were taken completely by surprise when it was used to blast into their armored tanks! But they soon developed their own bazooka, which they called the Tank Terror.

The most important rockets in World War II were huge weapons that flew for hundreds of miles before flattening their target. The Germans had the V2 rocket, which was one of the most terrifying weapons of the war. Thousands of V2s fell on England during the war, causing enormous damage.

After World War II, some scientists realized that if a rocket could fly along for 125 miles (200 km), then it should be able to fly up into the sky that far as well. Four people were central in designing a rocket that could fly that far up and take us to the moon.

The Rocket Researchers

Part I: The United States, 1926

American space scientist Robert Goddard got the rocket bug when, at age sixteen, he read the novel *War of the Worlds*, in which horrible Martians invade Earth and blast everyone to pieces. He began to dream of finding a way to get to Mars himself.

In 1908, Goddard started experimenting on rockets. He was the first person to show that a rocket could fly when there was no air, just like in space.

Goddard also changed the fuel that his rockets used. Early rockets used solid fuel. But Goddard knew that to get to the moon, an enormous amount of fuel would be needed. There would also be a big problem in space because there is no air. Fuel in cars and airplanes needs oxygen from the air to burn properly, but fuel in rockets needs to have its own oxygen supply, or the rocket will fizzle out and sputter back to Earth. Goddard made an important decision. To get to the moon, he decided, rockets needed to carry not solid fuel, not even gas fuel, but liquid fuel. And he was right. In 1926, he launched the world's first liquid-powered rocket from his Aunt Effie's farm. It just barely got off the ground, but that didn't matter—the point was that it worked.

Why Can't the Fuel Be a Gas? . . . .

A rocket needs to burn an immense amount of fuel to get into space. The molecules in a gas are much farther apart than they are in a liquid. This means that if you use liquid fuel, you pack more molecules in the same space than you would if you stored it as gas.

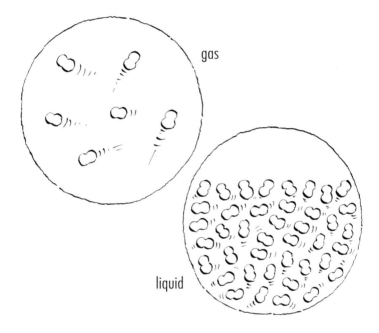

gas

liquid

In the first rockets that reached the moon, the fuel was liquid hydrogen and liquid oxygen. This burns very easily and makes water as a waste product. The liquid hydrogen had to be kept in a separate fuel tank, so that it didn't burn until it was supposed to.

The inside of a liquid-fuel rocket looks like this.

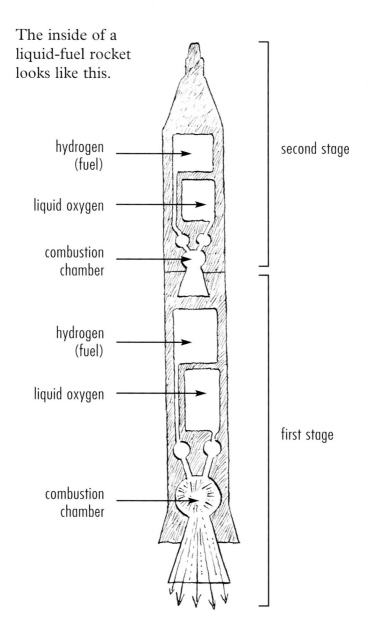

hydrogen (fuel)

liquid oxygen

combustion chamber

second stage

hydrogen (fuel)

liquid oxygen

combustion chamber

first stage

The liquid oxygen and hydrogen are pumped into a special combustion chamber, where they burn.

The Rocket Researchers

Part I, continued:

The United States, 1930s

Goddard eventually got some people interested in his rockets, and they agreed to give him some money to continue building them—to the amusement of everyone else! He was nicknamed "Moony" Goddard, and each of his rocket launches made him a laughing-stock...

That thing'll never get to the moon!

Yeah— it's got as much chance as the eagles' wings idea!

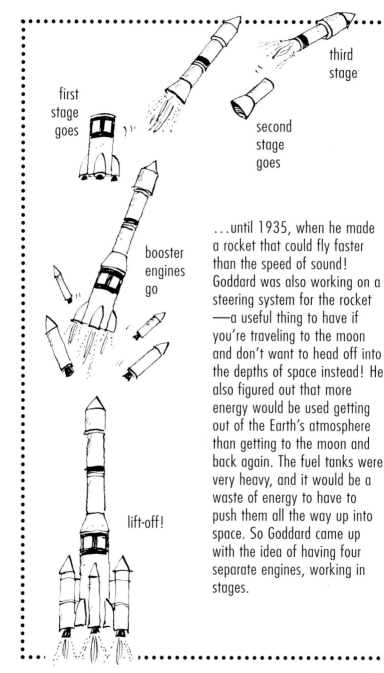

third
stage

first
stage
goes

second
stage
goes

booster
engines
go

...until 1935, when he made a rocket that could fly faster than the speed of sound! Goddard was also working on a steering system for the rocket —a useful thing to have if you're traveling to the moon and don't want to head off into the depths of space instead! He also figured out that more energy would be used getting out of the Earth's atmosphere than getting to the moon and back again. The fuel tanks were very heavy, and it would be a waste of energy to have to push them all the way up into space. So Goddard came up with the idea of having four separate engines, working in stages.

lift-off!

55

This idea was used for the Apollo spaceships—the spaceships that did eventually reach the moon. Each Apollo spaceship was carried by a rocket called Saturn V, which was bigger than a ten-story building. The fuel in its tanks lasted for only 30 seconds before the stage dropped off the bottom of the rocket. (Watch out for the people below!) Then the second-stage engines took over. This managed to get the rocket over 112 miles (180 km) up, and when the fuel ran out, this stage dropped off as well. The third stage was the smallest part of the Saturn rocket, and this managed to get the rocket into Earth's orbit. After blasting the rocket toward the moon, this stage dropped off as well. The rest of the journey to the moon and back was powered by the engines in the spaceship itself.

Goddard launched the first liquid-fueled rocket in 1926. It flew only 184 feet (56 meters) at about 62 mph (100 km/h). This was far too slow to get into space, but Goddard knew it could be done.

Goddard kept working, and in 1935 he managed to get a rocket to go 1 mile (1.6 km) into the sky. Unfortunately, Goddard's work was largely ignored.

Revolutionary Rocket Design ....

There were other important changes to make to rocket design before rockets could fly to the moon and back. For example, the way the hot gas is pushed out of the rocket changes how fast it can go. Rockets all have nozzles at the bottom, shaped like an upside-down funnel.

Nozzles make the rockets more powerful. Rockets that go up in space need very large nozzles to reach supersonic speeds (speeds that are faster than the speed of sound).

Be a Rocket Scientist
FIND THE BEST NOZZLE FOR YOUR ROCKET

Hey! What are you doing?

You can experiment to see how changing the shape of a nozzle makes your rocket go farther.

WHAT YOU'LL NEED
- a long balloon
- a room
- a straw
- a pair of scissors
- the nozzle of a dishwashing-soap bottle
- a long piece of thread
- tape
- a clothespin
- some cardboard

WHAT TO DO
1. Tape the thread to the wall on one side of a room.
2. Cut a length of straw about 4 to 6 inches (10 to 15 centimeters) long and thread the straw onto the thread.
3. Tape the other end of the thread to the opposite wall.

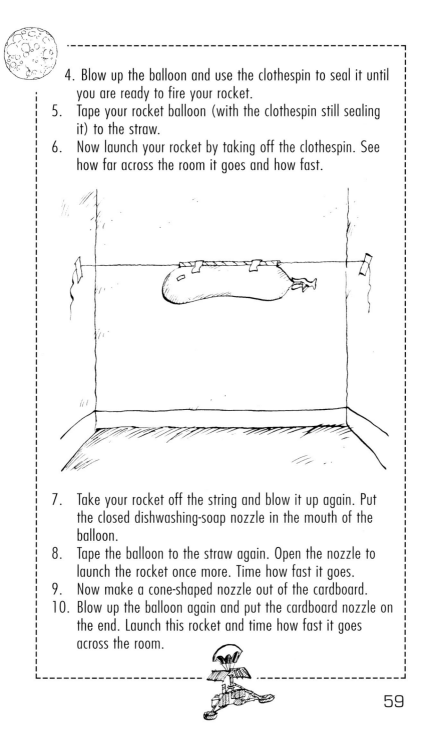

4. Blow up the balloon and use the clothespin to seal it until you are ready to fire your rocket.

5. Tape your rocket balloon (with the clothespin still sealing it) to the straw.

6. Now launch your rocket by taking off the clothespin. See how far across the room it goes and how fast.

7. Take your rocket off the string and blow it up again. Put the closed dishwashing-soap nozzle in the mouth of the balloon.

8. Tape the balloon to the straw again. Open the nozzle to launch the rocket once more. Time how fast it goes.

9. Now make a cone-shaped nozzle out of the cardboard.

10. Blow up the balloon again and put the cardboard nozzle on the end. Launch this rocket and time how fast it goes across the room.

The rocket balloon goes fastest when the air comes out through a narrow hole into a funnel-shaped nozzle. This is how all rockets have to be built. (You can try and find an even better nozzle shape if you want to!)

Balancing Your Booster ....

A rocket is more than a tube with nozzles. If you launched your rocket now, it would take off and fly all over the place, just as if you blew up a balloon and let go of it. That's not what you want at all. The rocket has to fly straight up into the air. You need something to stabilize the rocket and keep it on a steady course.

For hundreds of years, people used large sticks to balance their rockets. In the 1700s, the Indian army used rockets stabilized by 10-foot (3-meter)-long bamboo poles as weapons. The bamboo pole was almost as deadly as the rocket itself.

If you look at rocket fireworks, you'll see that they still use sticks to make them fly in a straight line. However, there are two main reasons why you can't use a big stick to stabilize a rocket to take you to the moon:

1. Your rocket has to be about 360 ft (110 m) high to carry enough fuel to get you into space. It would be very hard to find a stick that big!

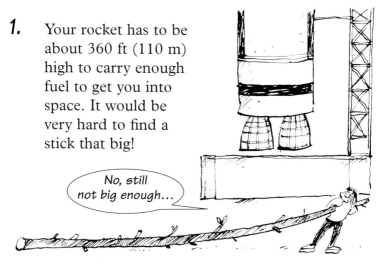

2. The rocket goes so fast through the air as it takes off that it would be very difficult to keep a stick stuck on. It would just blow off—even with superglue.

In the 1800s, William Hale, an English scientist, found a way to build war rockets without the guide-stick. He stuck flaps called vanes in the nozzle. This made the rocket fly in a straight line, but it also made it spin around as it flew!

In modern rockets, like the ones you'll fly to the moon, the vanes are on the outside of the rocket. They are controlled by a gyroscope—a fast-spinning wheel that you can't tilt, however hard you try. The gyroscope keeps the vanes in a position where the rocket is stabilized.

Be a Rocket Scientist
INVESTIGATE GYROSCOPES

WHAT YOU'LL NEED
- a bicycle wheel
- a friend
- two pairs of thick gloves (gardening gloves are ideal)

WHAT TO DO

1. Put on the gloves and hold the wheel in both hands by the axle.
2. Try tilting the wheel from one side to the other. How easy is it?
3. Hold the wheel upright again and ask your friend to put his or her gloves on.
4. While you hold the wheel, have your friend spin it by pulling down on the tire.
5. When the wheel is spinning very quickly, try to tilt the wheel again.

WHAT HAPPENS?
When the wheel is still, it is very easy to tilt it to one side or the other. When the wheel is spinning, it is much harder to tilt. The heavier the wheel and the faster it is spinning, the harder it is to tilt. This is how the gyroscope on a rocket works. It spins so quickly that it is very difficult to tilt over. This keeps the rocket moving in a straight line.

The Rocket Researchers

Part II:

Russia, 1890s–1930s

Another important rocket scientist was a Russian named Konstantin Tsiolkovsky. Tsiolkovsky had a hard life. At the age of nine he caught scarlet fever and became deaf. When he was a student in Moscow, he had to teach himself and ate only stale bread so that he could buy books. He spent most of his life as a high school teacher and had a little basement where he could do his experiments in his spare time.

Get this thing out of my living room!

Tsiolkovsky was obsessed with flight and space travel. He built a wind tunnel out of odd bits and pieces of material to test the design of aircraft and rockets. He was also interested in how people would talk to alien creatures once they did get to other planets. More important, he agreed with Goddard that rockets should have liquid fuel. He also proposed satellites to orbit the Earth and space stations between each of the planets. He died in 1935, so you can see how far ahead of his time he was— but most of his work was sadly ignored.

The Rocket Researchers

Part III:

Austria and Hungary, 1920s–1930s

The third important rocket scientist was Hermann Oberth, who came from Transylvania. His book about rockets was published in Germany in 1923, although he had to pay for it to be published after it was rejected by the university he had sent it to. Oberth sent a design for a long-range, liquid-fueled rocket to the war ministry, which also laughed at his idea and said it was nothing but a fantasy.

Scientists and engineers may have ignored Oberth's work, but some writers loved it and set up a space travel society. This society experimented with many kinds of rockets but had little success. This could have been because at this time, Oberth didn't really know how to build a rocket. In 1928, he was asked to build a rocket for a space film. Unfortunately, it was a complete failure—and in his effort Oberth lost an eye.

Later on, Oberth did build some working rockets. He also managed to figure out the very complicated math that showed how fast a rocket would have to fly to escape Earth's gravity. He also found out how to pretend he was weightless—a useful thing to try out before you go into space! In 1940, Oberth became a German citizen and went to work for his former assistant, Wernher von Braun.

The Rocket Researchers

Part IV:

Germany, 1930s

Wernher von Braun was one of the most important rocket researchers. He became interested in rockets as a child, when he read Oberth's book on space and couldn't understand the math. He decided to work hard until he was the best in his class. Soon after he left school, he joined a space travel society and helped Oberth in his spare time. By the time World War II started, von Braun was working on developing very powerful and deadly rockets. The most famous rocket he worked on was the V2. By the time the war ended, the Germans knew more about building long-range rockets than any other country on Earth!

During the war, there was no time to test whether a V2 could fly into space. But at the end of the war, when von Braun's rocket team surrendered to the United States, the Americans immediately put von Braun to work on a missile-building program. At the same time, the Russians took over most of the German rocket-building factories. The race for space had begun!

CHAPTER FIVE

THE SPACE RACE

After World War II, scientists knew rockets could be fired into space. The work of all the rocket researchers had shown that. But a rocket had yet to be built that was large enough to carry enormous amounts of fuel, plus enough equipment, water, and air for people to get into space. The United States had the knowledge of von Braun and his crew. The Russians also had some good scientists and all the rocket-building equipment. Who would be the first to win the race? It took twelve years to find out, and it proved to be the most exciting race in history!

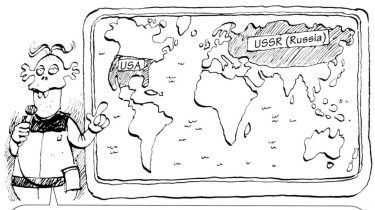

Here we are on planet Earth, where the backward species that call themselves humans are finally trying to get into space, only ten thousand years after we did! There are two teams—the Americans and the Russians. For some reason, they want to try and get to this dusty lump of rock with nothing on it called the moon. (They should try and visit the planet Zarg, which is much more interesting!)

To make things more difficult, and to keep them from cheating, the teams are separated by a screen called the Iron Curtain. This means they can't see what the other side is doing until their rockets are in space! Wait! They're off...

The Americans take off at high speed. They want to catch up with what the Germans managed to do with the V2. Oh! They've got a rocket 249 miles [400 km] into space! Wonderful! Now they're trying to figure out if they can put a nuclear bomb on a rocket... They can! But people aren't very impressed—they're very worried about the possibility of nuclear war, and this forces the Americans to slow down. Can the Russians catch up?

Yes, they can! The Russians have got a satellite called Sputnik I to orbit Earth.

The Americans are shocked. They don't know what to do...

...and it gets worse for them. The Russians have blasted another satellite up, this time with a dog inside! And the dog has survived in space! (Unfortunately, the poor thing is killed when the rocket falls back down to Earth and is burned up.)

The Russians just laugh. They've launched Luna I at the moon. The Americans hold their breath… but, phew! Luna misses and goes into orbit around the sun. The Russians claim this is the first artificial planet and call it Dream. (Ha! They haven't seen the artificial planet my people made—a thousand times bigger.)

The Americans can only sulk and stare in disbelief as the Russians try again. Luna II crash-lands on the moon. This proves that rockets can get there! Now this is getting silly. The Russians launch Luna III and they get it to go around the moon. It sends back pictures of the side of the moon that humans have never seen. (If they wanted to know what that side looked like, they could have asked us!) But where are the Americans? They're getting seriously left behind.

Now the Russians are pulling ahead even more. They've blasted a 5-ton rocket into space with a man named Yuri Gagarin inside. What a triumph! The Russians got the first man into space. Now the Americans are really worried. They've got to do something.

The Americans reply by blasting Alan Shepard into space. Now the race might get interesting. The Americans try again and get a man into orbit for 16 minutes.

The Russians just sneer and thumb their noses. They send a man into orbit for 25.6 hours. He goes around the Earth seventeen times. The Americans are trying very hard, but they just can't seem to do as well as the Russians. They got a man into orbit for only three times around the Earth. It looks like the Russians are going to win the race.

Now both runners are trying to see if humans can survive in space long enough to get to the moon and back. The Americans get Gordon Cooper to stay in space for 34 hours. But the Russians are miles ahead—they've got a woman in space, and she's been up there for 78 hours! Surely this is enough to win the race!

This is even more amazing: the Russians get a man to wander around in space in just his space suit—for 12 minutes!

But the Americans are making another superhuman effort. They manage to get a spaceship into space with two men in it—and keep them there for 190 hours. And they've made a clever backpack thing that pushes you around when you get out of your rocket. Oh dear, the Russians appear to be slowing down.

Hi!

But the Americans were getting too confident. The Russian spaceship Luna IX has landed on the moon safely! There is no one in it, but it looks as if it's all over for the Americans... Or is it? The Americans also get a spaceship to land on the moon. It sends back lots of pretty pictures. Then the Russians send another spaceship to the moon. It sends back information about the soil. And it looks like the Russians are also getting interested in Venus. They've sent a spaceship to Venus—and it's landed!

But now both sides have had terrible accidents. The Americans were testing a spaceship and it burst into flames. The three astronauts inside died. And the Russians have lost a cosmonaut. He was trying to get back into Earth's atmosphere, and his parachute lines became tangled up. He crashed to the Earth.

Moon Walking ....

So why didn't the Americans or Russians send people to the moon as soon as they knew a rocket could get that far?

Well, at the time, nobody knew how being in space for a long time would affect astronauts. They also didn't know whether the moon was safe to land on. This is why they landed unmanned spaceships on the moon first. With robots and computers, scientists tried to find out whether the soil was safe to walk on, whether the spaceship would sink into the soil when it landed, and where the safest place to land was. There was also a tiny chance that there were living creatures on the moon—and they may not have been too happy about us landing on it!

Besides, space is very dangerous for humans. Spaceships had to be designed that could carry two or three astronauts to the moon and back, along with enough air, water, and food to keep them alive.

This wasn't easy. It meant that the rockets had to be very big and heavy, so they had to be more powerful to get into space. However, once scientists had managed to land a few spaceships on the moon safely, they thought it should be possible to get the ships back home, too.

The disasters that struck both teams set back the race for space. The American mission was slowed down by a year, and the Russians' by two years. This gave the Americans the head start they needed.

And so the race continued...

Both teams have rested for a while and now it's time to start again. Now the Americans seem to be in the lead. They get two more spaceships onto the moon. They test the soil, and the scientists figure out that it is safe to walk on! But the spaceships that land have to stay there. I know humans are stupid, but I can't imagine anyone volunteering to go to the moon and never come back! What they need is to get a spaceship to go to the moon and back. Can they do it?

Yes! The Russians have done it! Their spaceship Zond 5 has traveled around the moon and come back to Earth... But what's this? The Americans pull ahead again! Saturn V has taken three astronauts around the moon and brought them back to Earth safely.

Where are the Russians now? They're testing out spaceships that can link up in space. They seem to have forgotten about the moon. And the Americans have won! They've gotten two men on the moon! The race is over.

Giving Up and Going Home....................

The Russians never did land people on the moon.
The Americans landed people on the moon six times,
most recently in 1972. Since then, not much has
happened. All there is to prove we have ever been
there is the equipment we left behind. All that effort
seems to have been for nothing. Why?

Well, the Americans stopped going to the moon
because it was too expensive. Instead, NASA has
concentrated on exploring other planets by sending
remote-controlled probes through the solar system.
We have discovered that Venus has a temperature of
1,650°F (900°C), so it would not be a very nice place
to visit. We also know there are no Martians on Mars,
and that Uranus, Neptune, and Saturn have rings.
NASA has also been putting money into developing
reusable spaceships such as the space shuttle, which
started flying in 1981. Because the shuttle can be used
over a hundred times and a rocket can
only be used once, space missions have
become cheaper. However, the space
shuttle was designed to carry satellites
and parts of space stations
into orbit. It cannot fly to the
moon, and it cannot land on
the rocky surface. A newly
designed, reusable rocket
will be needed
for that.

NASA
DESIGN
DEPT.

Now that scientists have discovered frozen water on the moon—and if we can crack the problem of designing a reusable rocket powerful enough to get there—it seems more likely that we will one day be able to set up a moon base. We now know that water will not have to be carried up there for people to drink and to grow food with. Water can also be used as fuel for spaceships because it can be split up into oxygen and hydrogen. Building a moon base would allow us to use the moon as a stepping stone to get to the other planets that we want to explore, such as Mars. But if you want to go there, you'll have to start training!

CHAPTER SIX

BLAST OFF ON YOUR MOON MISSION

Okay! Are you ready to go to the moon?

Step 1

To travel to the moon, you first have to satisfy the requirements for astronaut training. How do you match up to the astronaut checklist for the very first moon missions?

ASTRONAUT CHECKLIST, 1968
- MUST BE UNDER 40 YEARS OLD
- MUST BE NO TALLER THAN 5 FEET 11 INCHES
- MUST BE IN EXCELLENT PHYSICAL CONDITION
- MUST HAVE AN ENGINEERING DEGREE
- MUST HAVE FLOWN A PLANE FOR 1,500 HOURS (PREFERABLY A HIGH-SPEED JET)
- MUST **NOT** BE A WOMAN (ONLY THE RUSSIANS GOT A WOMAN INTO SPACE)

How are you doing so far? If you've failed that test, don't worry. Being an astronaut nowadays is a bit easier (as long as you don't want to be the pilot).

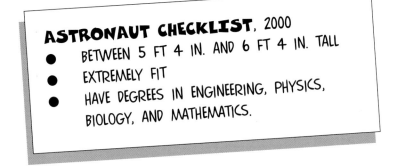

ASTRONAUT CHECKLIST, 2000
- BETWEEN 5 FT 4 IN. AND 6 FT 4 IN. TALL
- EXTREMELY FIT
- HAVE DEGREES IN ENGINEERING, PHYSICS, BIOLOGY, AND MATHEMATICS.

If you want to be a pilot, you'd have to fly a jet aircraft for over a thousand hours. (The U.S. Air Force would probably not appreciate your borrowing one of their planes for that long.) And as if that's not enough, all astronauts have to get extra training in meteorology, guidance and navigation, astronomy, physics, and computer science. (Now do you see why your teacher keeps bugging you about your homework?) If it all sounds too hard, don't give up! Perhaps you might be able to convince an astronaut training center that you're a child genius and your report card is really a college diploma...

First you will need zero-gravity training. This is difficult on Earth, but it can be done. A special aircraft is spun around. You will feel weightless for up to 30 seconds as you float.

You'll also be doing a lot of training underwater, because you're more buoyant there. (If you want to try this in the local swimming pool, don't wear a space suit—you'll get funny looks.)

Once you've gotten through zero-gravity training, you'll need to get suited up.

Step 2 ....

If you want to walk on the moon, you'll need a spacesuit—and you can't buy them in shops. Here's what you need to build your own:

Cool water running through tubes in your underwear to keep you from getting hot and sweaty. Otherwise your visor would steam up, and you wouldn't be able to see where you were going!

Clothes pumped full of air. This protects you from the difference in air pressure on the moon. Otherwise you'd get dizzy and fall over. The clothes also have to be jointed.

Just in case you get dizzy and fall over, cover your suit with a tough protective covering that won't rip. (If it does, you're in big trouble!)

The original moon astronauts had velcro attached to the inside of their visor so they could scratch their nose if it was itchy!

This box, called a Portable Life Support System, carries oxygen. Hoses carry the oxygen through to your suit. They also take away carbon dioxide when you breathe.

Boots, gloves, and a helmet. These must be attached to your spacesuit so that it is airtight. The visor on the helmet has a gold coating to protect you from the sun's rays.

83

Be a Rocket Scientist
SEE WHY YOUR SPACE SUIT
IS JOINTED

Your space suit needs to be pumped up with air, but this can make moving around very difficult. So your spacesuit has to be jointed. You can see why in this experiment.

WHAT YOU'LL NEED
● two long thin balloons
● some elastic bands

WHAT TO DO
1. Blow one balloon up very full.
2. Blow up the other balloon and slip two or three elastic bands on it to make it look like a string of sausages.
3. Try to bend each balloon, as if it were arms picking something up.

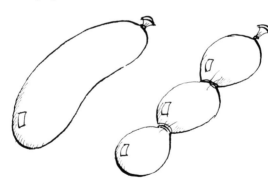

WHAT HAPPENS?
The balloon that is jointed bends much more easily than the one that isn't.

Answering the Call of Nature

Here's a problem. You're on the moon, jumping around, and suddenly you need to go to the bathroom. What do you do?

A. Take off your pants and find a rock to hide behind.

B. Cross your legs and try to hold on until you get back to your spaceship.

C. Wet yourself.

The answer is C! Well, not exactly. But you can't take your pants off on the moon—you would freeze, and all of the air would be sucked out of your space suit. So, before you put on your space suit, you have to put on a diaper! (Yes, all astronauts hate wearing them.)

Besides the space suit you wear in space and on the moon, you need another one for takeoff and landing. This one is bright orange, in case something goes wrong and you need to be seen by emergency services. It's a very special suit because it squeezes your legs. Without this suit, you would pass out when you took off or landed. The speeds you are moving at make the blood in your body behave in a very strange way. This suit keeps most of the blood where it should be—in the top of your body where it can get to your brain and not make your ankles swell up.

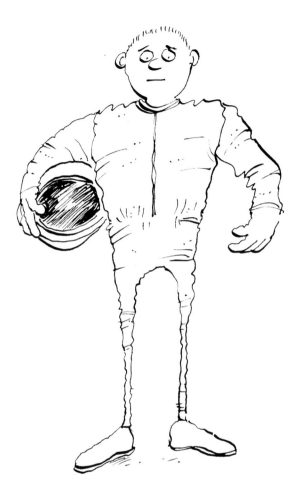

Step 3 ....

Now that you're outfitted with the right clothing, all you need is a rocket.

By now, you should know enough to be able to build a full-sized moon rocket. But if there isn't enough room for one in your backyard, you can try building this water-powered rocket out of dishwashing-soap bottles.

Be a Rocket Scientist
BUILD YOUR OWN
WATER-POWERED ROCKET

WHAT YOU'LL NEED

- 2 plastic dishwashing-soap bottles
- strong scissors
- a bicycle pump with an adapter for blowing up soccer balls
- a launchpad made from a sheet of plywood or cardboard leaning against something

WHAT TO DO

1. Take the nozzles off the bottles and wash everything. Leave it all to dry.
2. Cut the top and bottom off of one bottle. Keep the top piece, with its nozzle.

3. Cut the rest of the bottle up its side and flatten it out to make a sheet of plastic.

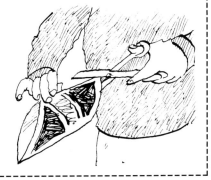

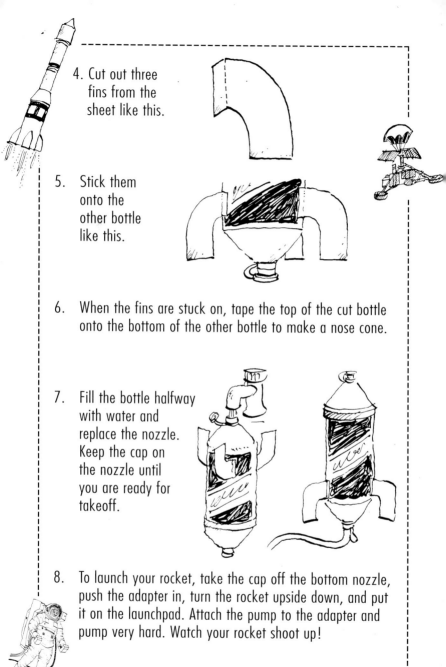

4. Cut out three fins from the sheet like this.

5. Stick them onto the other bottle like this.

6. When the fins are stuck on, tape the top of the cut bottle onto the bottom of the other bottle to make a nose cone.

7. Fill the bottle halfway with water and replace the nozzle. Keep the cap on the nozzle until you are ready for takeoff.

8. To launch your rocket, take the cap off the bottom nozzle, push the adapter in, turn the rocket upside down, and put it on the launchpad. Attach the pump to the adapter and pump very hard. Watch your rocket shoot up!

Step 4 ....

When you've got your rocket stages built, you have to get the whole thing ready for takeoff. Here's a handy checklist of what you'll need to prepare for takeoff.

TAKEOFF CHECKLIST

✳ A vehicle assembly building. This is a building where the three stages of the rocket and the command module (where you'll sit) are put together. The one for the original moon landing was the biggest building in the world—but you could use the garden shed.

Do you really need the lawn mower right now?

✳ A tower to hold the rocket upright when it's all put together. This should have an elevator in the side for you and your fellow astronauts to get up the 330 ft (100 m) to the command module.

✳ A heat-resistant launchpad. The heat from the rockets when you take off is so strong that it could set fire to a carpet 3 miles (5 km) away. (Let's hope you've got a BIG garden!)

✳ The most enormous pipes you can find, to pump the millions of gallons of fuel into the tanks of each rocket stage. You'll also need lots of people to help you do this.

✳ Computers to keep the rocket flying on the right course. Your home computer will be fine for this—it is far more powerful than the ones used on the first moon mission.

✳ An escape pod with parachutes attached in case something goes wrong. This will lift you out of any danger and bring you safely back to Earth.

✳ A command center with friends who can chat with you on the radio, see where you're going, and count down from ten so you know when to take off!

You and two friends are going to be living in your command module for over a week, so be sure to make it as comfy as possible. It's only a little bit bigger than a small car, and you've got to eat, wash, sleep, and work in it—no beds or sofas. If you want to stay safe on the way back to Earth, make sure you cover the outside of your command module with lots of heat-resistant layers. It's the only bit of the rocket that comes back to Earth, and when it falls into the atmosphere, it heats up so much that it becomes white-hot. Finally, attach a parachute to the module, so that you fall gently into the sea instead of splashing down so hard that you're flattened.

Put the command module right at the top of the rocket. Underneath it, you need to build a service module. This carries fuel, water, and oxygen, and has a little rocket that powers you back to Earth from the moon.

The top part of the command module is the lunar module. This is the only part of the rocket that will land on the moon. You need to make it out of aluminum so it will be light. There are two parts— a descent stage, which stays on the moon forever, and an ascent stage, which gets you back to the command module and home to Earth. The legs are in a honeycomb pattern (like in a beehive) to break the impact of landing. Cover the whole thing with another sheet of aluminum to protect you from any nasty meteorites that might come thudding into you!

Finally, why not build a car called a lunar rover? It should be really small and light, so that you can carry it in the lunar module. Wire wheels are best on the rocky, dusty lunar surface. Make sure you take some

That isn't much of a lunar rover.

navigational equipment or have your friend in the command module direct you from space, because everything on the moon looks almost the same. You could easily get lost. To power your car, you will need solar panels. You can find these on roofs for heating water and on solar-powered calculators.

Other things you might like to take with you:

* a flag, so people know you've been there
* a video camera
* golf clubs and balls—golf on the moon would be really fun!

Step 5 All Ready for Takeoff? ....

Takeoff will be the most frightening thing you'll ever do, and the noise will be the loudest sound you'll ever hear—so don't forget your earplugs! The takeoff speed pushes you back so hard that your face feels like jelly and wobbles around. (Luckily it doesn't stay like that afterward.) After a few minutes the pressure eases off, and if you undo your seatbelt, you will float up out of your seat. Look out the window—you're in space!

Step 6 ···

Congratulations—the rocket has reached the moon!
Now one of you must decide to stay in the command
module while the other two take the lunar module
down to the moon's surface.

When you've finally made it down to the moon, you'll
see that the scenery is a bit dull, but there are lots of
fun things you can do, such as

✳ making important speeches

✳ placing your flag in the dusty ground (you have to
   spread the flag out with wire, as there is no wind
   on the moon)

✳ jumping very high

✳ climbing high mountains with no effort at all

- driving your moon buggy
- collecting samples—don't go home without some moon rocks!

Step 7 ....

Time to head for home! Lift off in your lunar module and join up again with your colleague in orbit, before blasting off through space on your return journey to planet Earth.

So far, so good. But now you face one of the most dangerous parts of your moon mission—getting safely back through the Earth's atmosphere. As soon as your space capsule enters the Earth's atmosphere, it begins to fall so quickly toward the ground that friction from the air makes your rocket white-hot. Luckily, you've remembered to cover the outside of your rocket with a heatproof covering—haven't you?

Finally, if you kept falling all the way to the ground, you would be flattened! This is where your parachute comes in handy. (You did remember your parachute, didn't you?) Opening the parachute of your space capsule should slow you down enough to let you splash down into the sea, where you can be rescued.

So now you know how to build a rocket to get to the moon and what you need to survive there. No one has set foot on the moon since the Americans left it in 1972, but soon that might change. Several countries are working on a new international space station. They're also developing reusable rockets that slow down when they come back to Earth by using rotor blades on the side. Scientists are also planning a manned mission to Mars, which would be easier if people had a moon base. Less fuel would be needed to blast into space from the moon than from the Earth, and there wouldn't be as far to go.

The time will come when a moon base is built. When it does, you'll know how to build a rocket to get there, how to train as an astronaut, and what you're in for when you arrive.